AMAZING ART FORMS

The Art of Poetry

BY LAURA STICKNEY

Kids Core
An Imprint of Abdo Publishing
abdobooks.com

abdobooks.com

Published by Abdo Publishing, a division of ABDO, PO Box 398166, Minneapolis, Minnesota 55439. Copyright © 2025 by Abdo Consulting Group, Inc. International copyrights reserved in all countries. No part of this book may be reproduced in any form without written permission from the publisher. Kids Core™ is a trademark and logo of Abdo Publishing.

Printed in the United States of America, North Mankato, Minnesota.
102024
012025

THIS BOOK CONTAINS RECYCLED MATERIALS

Cover Photo: Galyna Motizova/Shutterstock Images
Interior Photos: Ground Picture/Shutterstock Images, 4–5; Wavebreak Media/Shutterstock Images, 7; B. O'Kane/Alamy, 8; Shutterstock Images, 10–11, 16, 28 (top), 29 (top), 29 (bottom); Jacob Wackerhausen/iStock/Getty Images Plus/Getty Images, 13; Red Line Editorial, 15; Kevin Winter/Getty Images Entertainment/Getty Images, 18; Stock Montage/Archive Photos/Getty Images, 20–21; Underwood Archives/Archive Photos/Getty Images, 23; Shawn Miller/Library of Congress/AP Images, 25; Jonathan Newton/The Washington Post/Getty Images, 26; Nattapol Sritongcom/Shutterstock Images, 28 (bottom)

Editor: Haley Williams
Series Designer: Katharine Hale

Library of Congress Control Number: 2024938336

Publisher's Cataloging-in-Publication Data

Names: Stickney, Laura, author.
Title: The art of poetry / by Laura Stickney
Description: Minneapolis, Minnesota: ABDO Publishing, 2025 | Series: Amazing art forms | Includes online resources and index.
Identifiers: ISBN 9781098295806 (lib. bdg.) | ISBN 9798384916802 (ebook)
Subjects: LCSH: Art--Juvenile literature. | Poetry--Juvenile literature. | Poems--Juvenile literature. | Poetry and the arts--Juvenile literature. | Poets--Juvenile literature. | Arts and history--Juvenile literature. | Poetry--Technique--Juvenile literature.
Classification: DDC 808.1--dc23

CONTENTS

CHAPTER 1
The Poetry Reading 4

CHAPTER 2
Poetry Basics 10

CHAPTER 3
The World of Poetry 20

Art Supplies 28
Glossary 30
Online Resources 31
Learn More 31
Index 32
About the Author 32

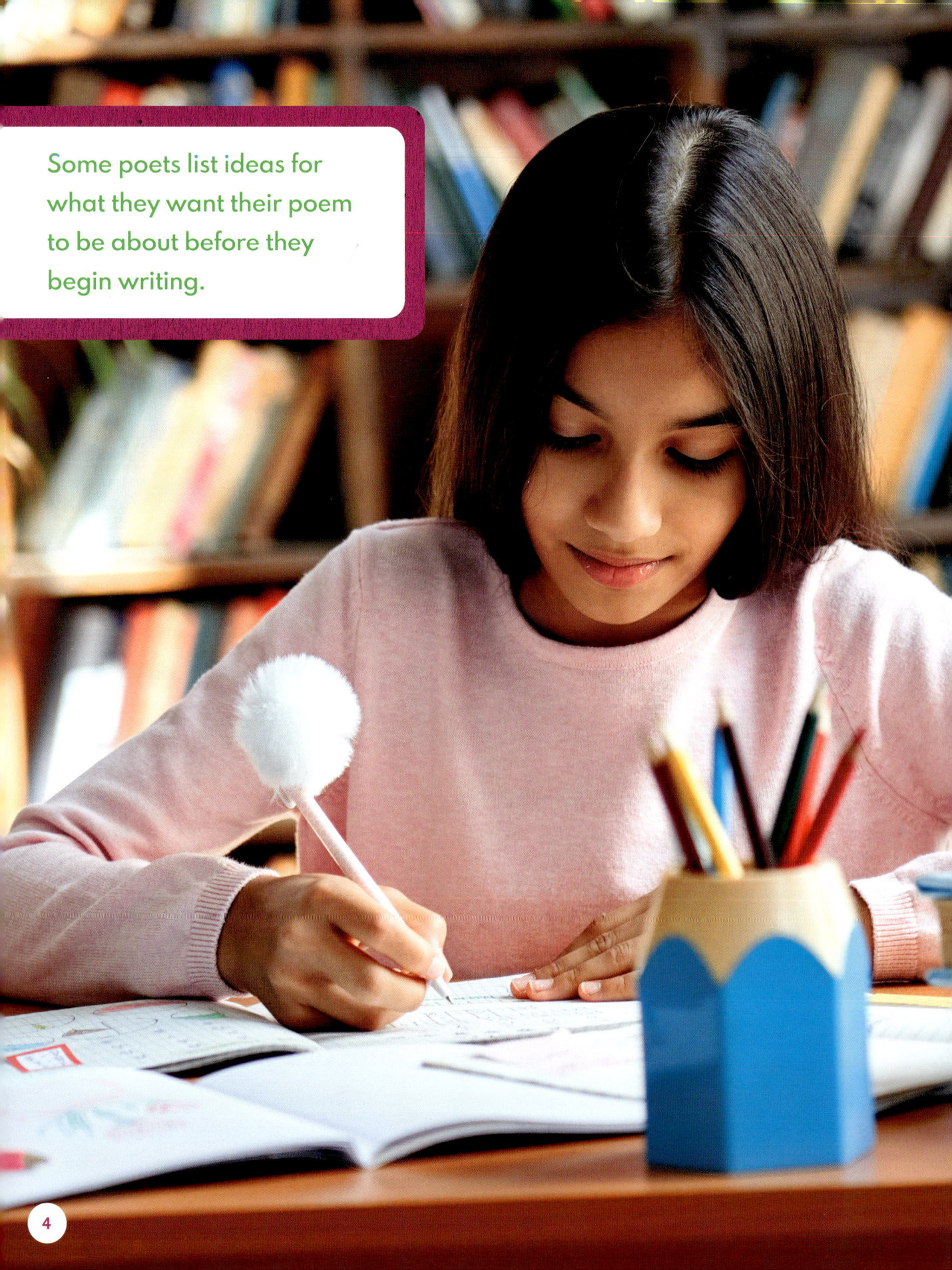

Some poets list ideas for what they want their poem to be about before they begin writing.

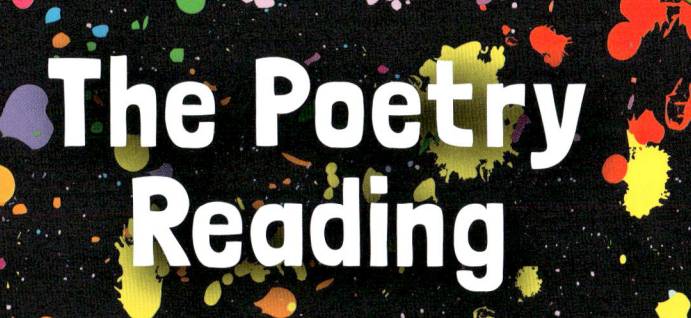

The Poetry Reading

Sylvia sat at her desk in her bedroom. She had a notebook and pen. Her class was learning about poetry at school. Each student had to write a poem.

Sylvia wasn't sure what to write about. She brainstormed ideas. Sylvia really liked baking.

It was her favorite thing to do with her grandma. She decided to write a poem about baking.

Sylvia began to write. She chose words to explain how she felt. She wrote about the smell and taste of sugar cookies. And she included details about her grandma. When she finished writing, Sylvia read her **draft**. She liked it, but

Ancient Art Form

Poetry has been around for thousands of years. Historians believe early poems were sung like songs. Some of these poems were epics. These are long poems that tell stories. One of the oldest is the *Epic of Gilgamesh*. It was written in Mesopotamia, or present-day Iraq. The poem is almost 4,000 years old.

Reading poetry can inspire people to write their own poems.

thought it could be better. So she edited the poem. Sylvia worked hard to get the words right. Finally, her poem was ready.

The next day, it was time for Sylvia to share her poem. She went to the front of the class.

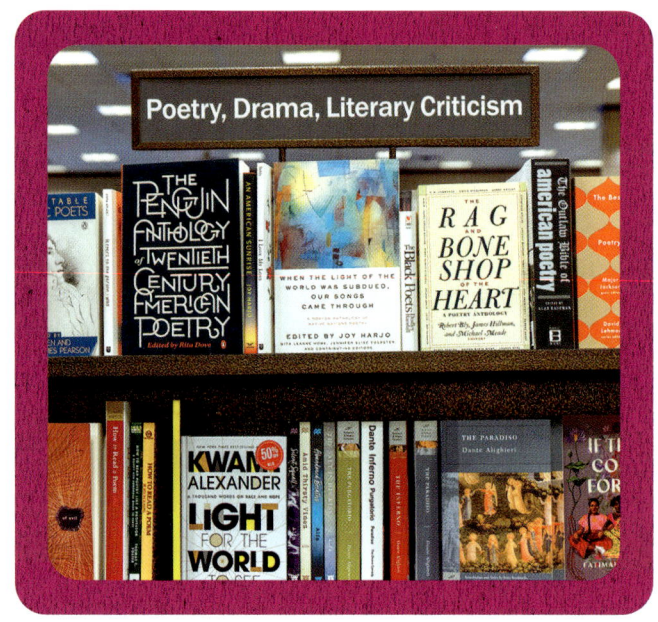

Bookstores and libraries often have sections specifically for poetry books.

She felt nervous. But she wanted to make her grandma proud. Sylvia cleared her throat and started reading. When she finished, her teacher and classmates clapped. Sylvia smiled. She couldn't wait to start writing more poems.

What Is Poetry?

Poetry is an art form. It is a type of **literature**. A poem is a creative arrangement of words. The words are usually in lines. Poems are often shorter than books or stories. People who write poems are called poets. Poets focus on the sound and rhythm of words. They use creative language to express feelings or form images.

Poetry takes on many forms. Poems do not always look or sound the same. No matter which form a poet chooses, the possibilities of poetry are endless.

Explore Online

Visit the website below. What new information did you learn about poetry that wasn't in Chapter One?

Poetry

abdocorelibrary.com/art-of-poetry

Poets often play around with words to express different ideas and emotions.

CHAPTER 2

Poetry Basics

Writing poetry requires only a few materials. Some poets write with a pencil or pen. They need paper or a notebook to write on. Others type their poems on a computer. Poets think creatively and experiment with their words.

They may use a dictionary or thesaurus to help them find new words to use.

Sound and Meter

Poetry uses several basic parts and techniques. Many poems focus on the sound of words. Poets use these sounds to create moods or feelings. A poem that uses "dr" and "br" might create a drum-like sound. Using "sh" may create a whispering sound.

Poets may also use alliteration, or repeating consonant sounds. An example of this is "she sells seashells by the seashore." Assonance is a similar technique. It involves repeating vowel sounds. One example is "the rain in Spain."

Reading a poem out loud can make it easier for an audience to hear different sounds and rhythms.

Some poets use rhymes, or words with similar sounds. "June" and "moon" are words that rhyme. Poets may follow patterns of rhyming words. Many nursery rhymes and popular songs use rhymes.

Poets sometimes make patterns with **syllables**. Words with one syllable are stressed. Words with more than one syllable have at least one stressed syllable. For example, the word *horseshoe* has two syllables. The first is stressed. The second is unstressed.

Poets may use a pattern of one unstressed and one stressed syllable. This pattern of syllables is called a foot. Poets may also use a pattern of feet within a line. A pattern of feet is called meter.

Poetic Meters

Meter Type	Pattern	Example
Iamb	unstressed / stressed	To**day** I **had** an **aw**ful **day**.
Trochee	stressed / unstressed	**Lit**tle **mon**key **threw** an **app**le.
Spondee	stressed / stressed	**Downtown bus stop**.
Anapest	unstressed / unstressed / stressed	It is **good** to be **glad**.
Dactyl	stressed / unstressed / unstressed	**Here** in the **gar**den it **rains** a lot.

The most common types of poetic meter use patterns of two or three syllables. Patterns may be repeated throughout a line in order to create a rhythm.

Figurative Language

Poems use language to create feelings or images. This is known as figurative language.

The word *splash* is a type of figurative language called onomatopoeia. Onomatopoeia is when a word describing a sound resembles the sound itself.

Similes compare things using *like* or *as*. An example of that is "busy as a bee." Metaphors also compare things, but without using *like* or *as*.

Another type of figurative language is personification. Personification is used to talk about a nonhuman thing as if it were human. A poet might write "the moon went to sleep."

Poets also use imagery. This involves using senses to create clear images. A poet may describe the touch, taste, or smell of something.

Poetry Forms

There are many forms of poetry. Free **verse** poems do not rhyme. They also do not follow a pattern. Concrete poems are arranged to form shapes. **Prose** poems are written with no line breaks. The haiku is a Japanese poetry form.

Spoken Word Poetry

Spoken word poetry is a modern poetry form. It is meant to be read out loud and is often performed on a stage. Spoken word poets focus on sound, rhythm, and wordplay. They may use music and dance while reading their poem. Poets sometimes compete in poetry slams, also called spoken word contests.

Famous poet Amanda Gorman is best known for her poem "The Hill We Climb."

Haikus have three lines. Lines one and three have five syllables. Line two has seven syllables.

Most poems are made up of stanzas. Stanzas are groups of lines. They are typically separated from other stanzas on a page.

Stanzas can also have a different number of lines. A four-line stanza is called a quatrain. A two-line stanza is a couplet.

Poets decide when and where to end each line. They may use enjambment. This is when a line or phrase runs over into the next line without any punctuation.

Further Evidence

Look at the website below. Does it give any new evidence to support Chapter Two?

9 Different Types of Poetry

abdocorelibrary.com/art-of-poetry

William Shakespeare was known for writing 14-line poems called sonnets.

The World of Poetry

Poetry has a long history. It has changed a lot over time. During the 1400s and 1600s, poems usually followed traditional forms. Most focused on topics of love and religion. Famous poets such as William Shakespeare were popular during this time.

In the 1800s, American poets such as Emily Dickinson and Walt Whitman wrote about new topics. They explored life, nature, and death. During the 1920s, Black American poets such as Langston Hughes wrote about their lives and experiences.

Later poets, such as Sylvia Plath and Elizabeth Bishop, embraced new forms and topics. Others were inspired by music

Modernism

One era of poetry was Modernism. In the early to mid-1900s, poets wanted to break away from traditional forms. They experimented with new ideas. Major Modernist poets include T. S. Eliot, Gertrude Stein, Wallace Stevens, and William Carlos Williams.

Langston Hughes wrote during a period known as the Harlem Renaissance. One poem he wrote is titled "Harlem."

and politics. Poems from the past continue to have a big effect today. They shape how people think about and write poetry.

Poetry Today

Today, poets write in a wide variety of forms and styles. Some write about politics and **human rights**. Poets might share their writing on social media. They may also give poetry readings or host book-launch parties.

Many poets enter contests or submit poetry books to publishers. They try to get their work published. Others send poems to literary magazines. Some poets earn prizes for their work. One example is the Yale Series of Younger Poets Prize.

Each year, the Library of Congress chooses a Poet Laureate. This title is given to a poet who shows poetic greatness. In 2022, Ada Limón became the US poet laureate. Other major

Ada Limón was selected for a second term as the US poet laureate from September 2023 to April 2025.

modern poets include Amanda Gorman, Terrance Hayes, and Ocean Vuong.

Organizations and Events

Many organizations support poets. The Academy of American Poets is based in New York City. It holds poetry **workshops**. The Poetry Foundation is a literary organization and publisher. It hosts events, awards, and contests. It also publishes *Poetry* magazine.

Joining writing groups and going to poetry readings are great ways for new poets to get involved in the art form.

Several poetry events happen throughout the year. April is National Poetry Month. Some groups, such as Button Poetry, host annual poetry slams. Poetry festivals are also popular events. The Geraldine R. Dodge Poetry Festival is the biggest one in North America.

Poetry comes in many forms. Poets continue creating new ideas every day. That is why so many people around the world enjoy poetry.

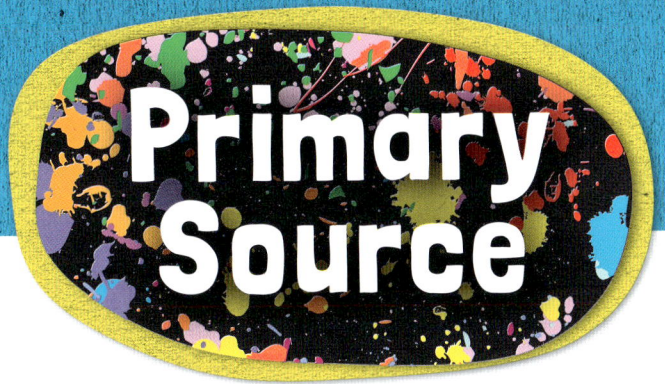

In 2022, US Poet Laureate Ada Limón spoke about the role of modern poetry:

> There has been a push over the last ten years to make poetry accessible. It's not always in the classroom. Sometimes it's on the subway. Sometimes it's on social media. . . . That kind of access has ignited a passion, not only to read poetry, but to write it.

Source: Olivia B. Waxman. "Ada Limón Talks about Poetry's Role." *Time*, 16 Oct. 2022, time.com. Accessed 26 Feb. 2024.

What's the Big Idea?

What is this quote's main idea? Explain how the main idea is supported by details.

Art Supplies

Pencil or pen

Notebook

Computer

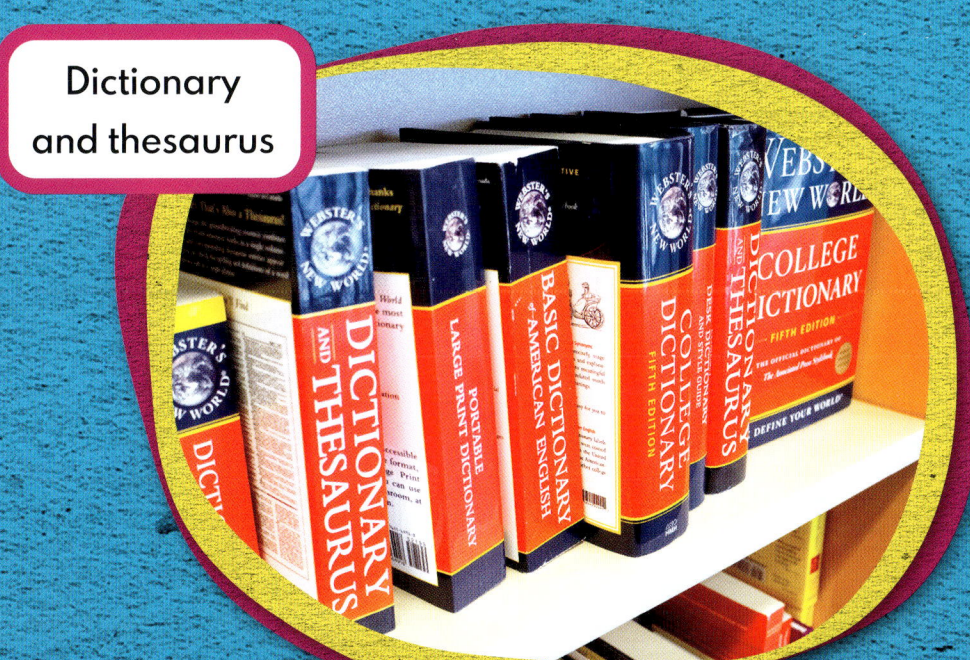

Dictionary and thesaurus

Glossary

draft
the first, unedited version of a piece of writing

human rights
the freedoms and liberties people have no matter their race, ethnicity, religion, or gender

literature
written works, such as books, poetry, or plays

prose
a form of writing that sounds like normal speech

syllable
a part of a word made up of a single sound

verse
a form of poetic writing that can be arranged using lines, meter, and rhythm

workshops
gatherings in which writers discuss and give feedback on writing

Online Resources

To learn more about poetry, visit our free resource websites below.

Visit **abdocorelibrary.com** or scan this QR code for free Common Core resources for teachers and students, including vetted activities, multimedia, and booklinks, for deeper subject comprehension.

Visit **abdobooklinks.com** or scan this QR code for free additional online weblinks for further learning. These links are routinely monitored and updated to provide the most current information available.

Learn More

A World Full of Poems. DK, 2020.

Coelho, Joseph. *Poems Aloud.* Wide Eyed Editions, 2020.

Van Oosbree, Ruthie, and Lauren Kukla. *Haiku Poems.* Abdo, 2023.

Index

Epic of Gilgamesh, 6

festivals, 26
figurative language, 15–16

Hughes, Langston, 22

imagery, 9, 15–16

Limón, Ada, 24, 27
literary magazines, 24–25

materials, 5, 11–12
meter, 14–15
Modernism, 22

patterns, 14–15, 17
poetry forms, 9, 17, 21–22, 24, 26
poetry slams, 17, 26

rhyme, 14, 17

Shakespeare, William, 21
sound, 9, 12–14, 17
spoken word poetry, 17
stanzas, 18–19

Yale Series of Younger Poets Prize, 24

About the Author

Laura Stickney is a poet, editor, and artist from the Twin Cities area in Minnesota. She is currently pursuing a master of fine arts degree in poetry. Her favorite poets are Emily Dickinson, Sylvia Plath, and Matthea Harvey.